READ WHAT CAN HAPPEN WHEN YOU

Never Give Up and Go For It!

LETTERS FROM INSPIRATIONAL HEROES

ANDY ANDREWS, AUTHOR OF *STORMS OF PERFECTION*™

Dedicated to the children and parents of
The Big Oak Ranch in Ft. Payne, Alabama. You inspire us all!
Special thanks to Ben and Jackie Peters for introducing me to Dalmatian Press.

This children's book series is based on the
Andy Andrews book series *Storms of Perfection.*™

Publisher, Producer: Chris Hilicki
Cover Illustration: Kevin Menck, Text Illustrations: Jerry Dillingham
Art Direction: Andy Mangrum, Photos of Andy Andrews: Peter Nash

ISBN: 1-57759-778-8

First Published in the United States in 2002 by Dalmatian Press, LLC.

11856

02 03 04 QWB 10 9 8 7 6 5 4 3 2 1

Table of Contents

Michael W. Smith

Entertainer

As a boy, Michael W. Smith loved music. He liked to sing and play music with his friends. After high school, he made some bad decisions. He hung out with the wrong kids. Then he remembered the faith he had when he was younger. His faith helped him make the right decisions.

He started his life again in a new direction. He started writing and singing songs.

He said, "I WILL HELP PEOPLE HAVE FAITH." He wrote happy songs about his faith. His friend, Amy Grant, liked his music. She recorded one of his songs. That made him famous!

Now he has had 21 number one songs of his own. His records have sold millions of copies. His happy life is music to everyone's ears!

DO YOU LIKE TO SING?

HOW MANY SONGS WILL YOU WRITE IN YOUR LIFE?

GO FOR IT!

In Their Own Words

Michael W. Smith

Dear Andy,

I played shortstop on a Little League team. It was one of the worst teams our town had ever seen. That was funny because our coach was really talented. He could have played in the major leagues. He was my hero. After all, he was my dad.

Our record was a perfect 0 and 15! You might think that Dad would get discouraged. But he never got upset. He loved us very much. In our league, there was a tradition that if you won a ball game, your whole team got ice cream to celebrate. But Dad had a new idea. He said, "Boys, don't ever give up." Then he smiled. He said, "We'll get 'em next time!" Then he bought us ice cream to celebrate our loss.

Well, guess what? We won our very last game! You'd have thought we'd won the World Series! We shouted all the way to the ice cream stand that night. When I think about that time, I never feel bad about playing for a losing team. My dad taught me what he had learned from his heavenly Father. Win or lose, I can always go to God because He is my Father. He loves me unconditionally. When you realize how much He believes in you, you'll want to open your heart and talk to Him.

Sincerely,

Michael W. Smith

Bobby Bowden

NCAA Football Coach

Bobby Bowden is a friend and role model. And he is one of our country's favorite college football coaches. He gives time to charities and his church. He always has a wink and a smile for a kid. He knows that people need to be encouraged. That's because there were times in his life when **he** needed it.

Bobby never got jobs he applied for. Instead, every job he had was offered to him out of the blue! People said,

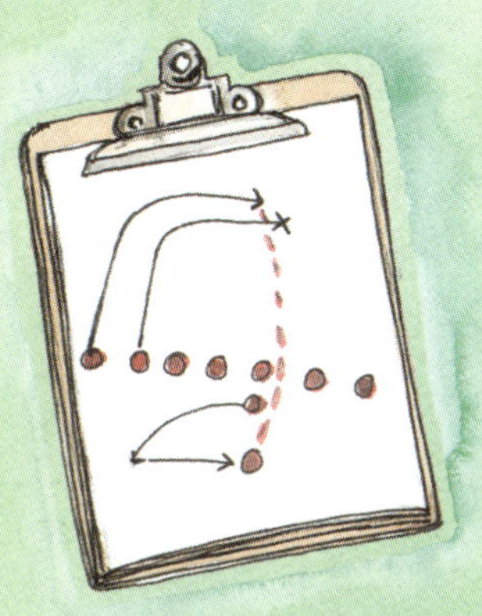

"WE WANT YOU TO BE OUR COACH!"

He is now the head coach of the Florida State football team.

He has won a lot of important football games. He has won more games than almost every other college football coach!

HAVE YOU EVER BEEN TURNED DOWN FOR SOMETHING?

HOW MANY GAMES WILL YOU WIN IN YOUR LIFE?

GO FOR IT!

In Their Own Words

Dear Andy:

My life consists of example after example of failure, followed by success, and rejection followed by acceptance. Any time I fail I get excited that something great is going to happen. At the age of thirteen, I was withdrawn from elementary school for eight months because of Rheumatic fever. I had to lay flat on my back. It was during this isolation from school, church and playmates that my lifetime direction was mapped out. It was during this time that I stopped to 'listen!'

One day I lay flat on my back. My mother asked me, "Bobby, do you believe in prayer?" I said yes. She said, "Do you think GOD can answer prayer?" I said yes. I prayed. HE answered. HE restored my soul and gave me my direction in life…Serving HIM through football.

My sophomore year in high school, I broke my hand in practice before the first game. I couldn't play. I grew from my junior year to my senior year. I gained enough weight to be offered a football scholarship.

Every job I applied for in coaching, I was 'rejected.' I never got a coaching job I applied for. Darn if God didn't get me better jobs than the ones I applied for and was turned down. It all began back when I stopped to 'listen' to God and my mother.

Sincerely,

Coach Bowden

Bobby Bowden
Head Football Coach

Candy Lightner

Author and Speaker

Candy Lightner has made a wonderful difference in people's lives. But one time, an awful thing happened to her. Her daughter, Cari, was killed by a drunk driver. At first Candy was very sad. Then she got angry. She decided to turn her anger into something good, and help people.

She found out that the laws let a lot of drunk drivers go free. She talked to the people who made the laws. She said, "I WANT TO GET DRUNK DRIVERS OFF THE ROADS."

She started a group called Mothers Against Drunk Driving.

The laws were changed. She has made our country a safer place for all of us.

HAS SOMETHING HAPPENED IN YOUR LIFE THAT MADE YOU SAD AND ANGRY?

CAN YOU HELP OTHER PEOPLE BY SHARING WHAT YOU LEARNED DURING THAT TIME?

GO FOR IT!

In Their Own Words

AMERICANS AGAINST CRIME

Dear Mr. Andrews,

Most people do not think I lead a "charmed life." My obstacles have been well publicized starting with the death of my daughter, Cari, by a drunk driver in 1980.

I don't view rejection as failure, but as a learning experience. I started MADD. I began the anti-drunk driving movement. Imagine my shock when I discovered that saving lives was a political issue and not a human one.

My first day was frustrating. We were attempting to pass tougher laws against drunk driving. The first legislator I visited wouldn't even see me. His aide told me his boss felt the laws on the books were adequate. At that time, impaired drivers were receiving nothing more than a slap on the wrist.

The second legislator told me that if I didn't like the way this country was run, I should leave it. Not change it, leave it. A third legislator proceeded to take a phone call in the middle of my conversation! I never felt more angry and determined in all my life.

Well our bills passed. Lives have been saved. Attitudes have changed. MADD taught me more than how to speak before an audience and run a corporation. It taught me that one person can make a difference.

Sincerely,

Candy Lightner

Candy Lightner

Norman Vincent Peale

Minister and Author

There is a very famous book called "The Power of Positive Thinking." It is the first book written by Norman Vincent Peale. He wrote over 40 other books. But his first one was almost his last one! When the book came out, critics did not like it. They said it was full of dumb ideas.

But he did not listen to the people who said bad things about him. He listened to his heart. And he listened to the people who loved him. They said, "YOU NEED TO KEEP WORKING."

His book has now sold more than 22 million copies. Wow, that's a lot of books! I wonder what his critics think of that!

The President of the United States gave him a special medal. It is called the Medal of Freedom. That's a pretty big deal!

DO YOU ENCOURAGE YOUR FRIENDS?

WOULD YOU LIKE TO WRITE A BOOK?

GO FOR IT!

In Their Own Words

Norman Vincent Peale

Dear Andy:

I suffered rejection when I wrote a book called *The Power of Positive Thinking.* It hit the best seller lists. It was on the New York Times best seller list for 186 weeks. This projected me into the most criticism I ever received. I considered the book a Christian book. But some ministers preached against some terrible thing labeled "Pealism." This became so violent that I actually wrote out my resignation from the ministry. Though my church stood by me.

I took a train to see my father. He said, "Norman, you have always been true and loyal to Jesus Christ. You believe in and preach Bible truths. Your old father has known good men and not so good men, both in and out of church. You are a good and loyal minister of Jesus Christ." He was silent for a long minute. "Besides, the Peales never quit. It would break my heart if one of my sons was a quitter." I tore up my resignation and threw it in the wastebasket.

The book has sold upwards of 20 million copies worldwide. The title has become part of the language. In every rejection you learn something. I learned that if you love people and not hate anyone that you gain a victory.

Cordially yours,

Norman Vincent Peale

Norman Vincent Peale

Daniel “Rudy” Ruettiger

Motivational Speaker

Rudy Ruettiger had a lot of people tell him he couldn’t do things when he was young. His teachers said that he was not very smart. People told him that he was too poor to go to college. They said he was not big enough to play football.

But he said, "I CAN LEARN IF I WORK HARD." He did not give up on his dreams. If you want to know the whole story, you can watch a great movie about him! It is called "Rudy." He is a symbol of what can happen if you work hard and never give up.

He did go to college and play football. In fact, at the end of his last game, he was carried off the field like a hero while the crowd chanted his name!

WHAT ACTOR WILL STAR AS YOU IN THE MOVIE OF YOUR LIFE?

WOULD YOU LIKE TO HEAR PEOPLE CHANTING YOUR NAME?

GO FOR IT!

In Their Own Words

Rudy

"Never Give Up On Your Dreams"

Dear Andy,

We all have dreams as children. With me those dreams revolved around Notre Dame football. But to get into that University your grades have to be top notch. My teachers told my parents that I was not very bright. My parents believed them. I also believed for a time that I was stupid. I found out later that I had a learning disorder. I wasn't stupid at all!

I applied to Notre Dame. I was rejected. But I learned patience. I applied and was rejected every semester. I kept applying. Finally, I was accepted. I did go on to play football for Notre Dame, then made the movie, *Rudy*. The process in reaching any dream is the same. Focus on your dream. Understand the steps to get it. Then never—ever—ever let it go.

I remember the day my little league coach took the team to a big league game. He caught a foul ball and asked, "Who wants it?" Everybody wanted it. He said that after the game we'd stop off at the little league field. He'd hit it into the outfield. Whoever got it first could have it. I don't remember the rest of the game. I replayed a vision of me getting the ball. When the time came, I got the ball. That is still a big deal to me.

I guess the question is, "Who wants it?" Dream Big Never Quit!

Daniel Rudy Ruettiger

Daniel "Rudy" Ruettiger

Cheryl Prewitt Salem

Former Miss America

Many girls dream of being Miss America. But each year, only one young lady gets to wear the crown. Cheryl Prewitt Salem never had a good chance of being Miss America. Her family was poor. They couldn't buy pretty clothes.

MISSISSIPPI

Being poor wasn't her only problem. There were a lot of times when she could have felt sorry for herself. She could have said, "I GIVE UP ON MY DREAM." But she made it to the Miss America competition. She even lost five years in a row before she won!

Today, she is an author. She talks to people about her faith. She shows people how to not give up hope.

WHAT DO YOU DREAM OF DOING
WHEN YOU GROW UP?
HOW MANY PEOPLE
WILL YOU ENCOURAGE?
GO FOR IT!

In Their Own Words

C P Annie Productions, Inc.

Dear Andy:

I was born in Mississippi and lived on a dirt road outside of a town that did not even have a local beauty pageant! My wardrobe consisted of dresses we could make from flour sacks.

Had that been my only opposition life would have been almost a breeze. But a car accident when I was 11 years old left my face with over 100 stitches. My back was cracked. My left thigh bone was smashed.

That's when I realized life is a series of CHOICES. I *chose* to believe that I *would* walk again someday. The day came for the cast to be removed. My leg was stronger than any bone in my body. I could walk! I knew it was a miracle. The same God who had formed that bone could take care of everything else…if I wouldn't give up!

So I'm all set to become Miss America. I am poor, I have scars on my face, crooked teeth, and emotional scars! But I had faith in God and in myself. That's all you need.

I continued to grow until I was at the place where the Lord needed me to be. I never quit. I knew that God created me to be a winner just as He has each of us. And when that day was here, I was ready to accomplish all that God had called me to do when I was crowned Miss America 1980.

Sincerely,

Cheryl Prewitt Salem

Cheryl Prewitt Salem

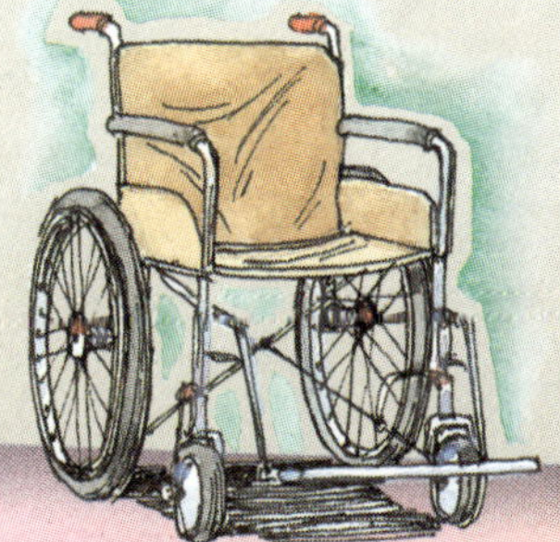

Dr. Robert H. Schuller

Minister and Author

Robert Schuller always knew he wanted to be a minister. First he went to college. Then he worked as a pastor at a church. A few years later, he and his wife started their own church. He rented a drive-in movie theater. He stood on the roof of the snack bar to give his sermons! Can you imagine that?

A lot of people laughed at him when he started his church. They said he would fail. He heard what they were saying about him. But he didn't listen! He told himself, **"NOTHING IS IMPOSSIBLE."**

Now his Sunday services are on TV. It is watched by more people than any other church service in the whole world!

HAS ANYONE EVER LAUGHED AT SOMETHING YOU WERE DOING?

DO YOU KNOW WHAT YOU WANT TO DO WHEN YOU GROW UP?

GO FOR IT!

In Their Own Words

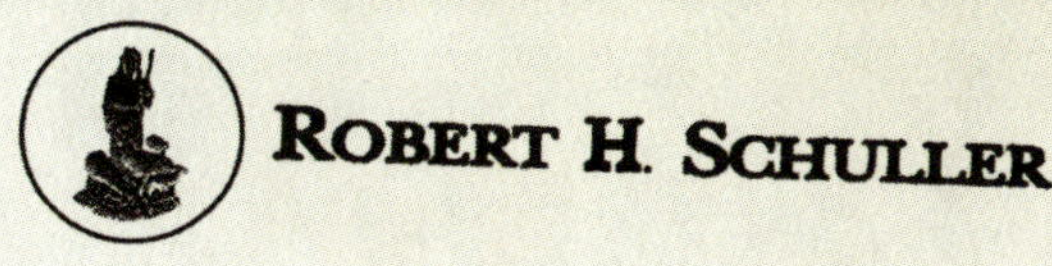

Dear Andy:

The storms in our lives shape us into what we become. This lesson was taught to me at a very early age.

I grew up on a small farm in Iowa. Although my parents were very poor, there was always food on the table, a warm place to sleep, and enough money to give to the church every week. My father began to teach me that with a little imagination and hard work, we could always get by.

One winter we couldn't afford to buy coal for the furnace. My father came up with a wonderful idea. Every morning the hogs were fed ears of corn. Then dad had me round up the leftover corncobs to use in the furnace. It kept our house warm all winter long!

As a pastor, I can't begin to tell you how many times I've heard, "It's impossible!" or "I can't do it!" The wonderful news I have for you is that "IT IS POSSIBLE!" God created each person with a special gift. It is up to us to discover our potential and turn obstacles into opportunities!

God loves you and so do I!

Robert H. Schuller

PHOTO BY: MIKE RUTHERFORD

Ricky Skaggs

Entertainer

Ricky Skaggs has a loving family. They all love music. He started playing music when he was just five years old! He knew he wanted to be a musician when he grew up. He knew that it would take a lot of practice to be good. So he played every day.

Sometimes he felt like doing things that were more fun. But he kept on practicing. He started his first band when he was 18. He signed a record contract when he was 27. He became a star. But he reminds people, "I PRACTICED EVERY DAY FOR 22 YEARS BEFORE I WAS FAMOUS!"

Sometimes things don't go right for him. But he knows that faith and a positive attitude help keep things on the right track!

WHAT DO YOU PRACTICE REGULARLY? HOW CAN YOUR FAITH AND ATTITUDE HELP YOU? GO FOR IT!

In Their Own Words

Dear Andy,

I would like to share a few things from my heart.

I came to Nashville in 1980. I was launched into super stardom within a year. In 1985, I was voted CMA Entertainer of the Year. Then in 1986, my son was shot by a drugged-out truck driver. At that moment I felt the lowest I've ever felt. I thought God had forgotten all the promises he had made me. But He proved His faithfulness! My son recovered.

Then my record sales started dropping off. Everyone else was having the big record sales, the big crowds, the movie offers…not me. I asked God, "Where are you?" I heard Him say, "I'll never leave you." So I got to thinkin', I believe this is a blessing from above. The Lord was trying to teach me to trust in Him for everything.

So I've been focusing my attention on family and friends. I'm happier now than I've ever been. I love music more now than ever before. I've seen how God has used my music to heal people. I know the changes I've gone through have all been for the best. I know that I won't let acceptance or rejection affect my music or my walk with God.

I know it takes storms in life to perfect us. I also know that I'm not perfect. But I'm glad to know that God loves me enough to stand by me when the storms come! He is faithful.

Ricky Skaggs

Ricky Skaggs

Patty Wetterling

Children's Rights Advocate

Patty Wetterling loves her family very much. She has a son named Jacob. One day, a very bad man grabbed Jacob. He took Jacob away. She does not know where Jacob is. But she decided not to sit around and cry. She wanted to do something good.

She said, "I WILL TRY TO HELP OTHER FAMILIES." She started the Jacob Wetterling Foundation. It is a group that helps keep children safe. They help search for missing kids. She teaches kids how to be safe. She teaches their parents, too.

She cares for Jacob very much. That is one of the reasons why she is making the world a safer place for all of us.

DO YOU KNOW WHAT TO DO IF A STRANGER TALKS TO YOU?

WHAT CAN YOU DO TO HELP SOMEONE WHO IS SAD?

GO FOR IT!

In Their Own Words

The Jacob Wetterling Foundation

Dear Andy,

On October 22, 1989, my son was kidnapped. For weeks I cried, I yelled, I walked around in a trance.

Having a missing child leaves people feeling frightened and sad. I remember one day saying, "I can't do this anymore. It's too hard." I had this vision of Jacob doing the same thing, echoing my thoughts with "They've given up. I'll never make it home." I found myself saying, "Hold on Jacob. Don't give up. Stay strong. I love you."

I made a decision. I will do anything to find Jacob and other missing children. I will fight to stop this from happening to other families. We circulated millions of Missing posters. We traveled the country to raise awareness of missing children. We fought for three years in Washington D.C. to help protect children. Finally, Congress passed the Jacob Wetterling Crimes Against Children Sex Offender Registration Act.

I know the value of dreams and never giving up. If we have no vision of what we hope will happen, how can we take the steps to get there? Never give up. Never forget. We are the hope for a safe future for children everywhere. Please hold our missing children in your hearts until we can hold them in our arms again.

Sincerely,

Patty Wetterling

Patty Wetterling
Jacob's mom

Jeanne White

Founder of the Ryan White Foundation

Jeanne White had a wonderful son named Ryan. He died many years ago. He got sick with something we call AIDS. It wasn't his fault. He got it from a bad blood transfusion. It happened before we really knew very much about AIDS. A lot of people did not understand the disease. They were afraid to be around Ryan and his family.

Ryan knew that people were scared. He learned to forgive them for being mean to him. He said, "I KNOW YOU ARE AFRAID BECAUSE YOU DON'T UNDERSTAND."

His mother was also forgiving. She knows that the more we understand about AIDS, the less we will be afraid of it. She also knows that one day we will find a cure for it.

Now she helps raise money to find a cure. She also teaches people about the disease. She likes helping people learn to not be afraid.

HAVE YOU EVER SEEN SOMEONE ACT MEAN TO A PERSON WHO IS SICK?

WHAT CAN YOU DO TO HELP A SICK PERSON FEEL LOVED?

GO FOR IT!

In Their Own Words

RYAN WHITE
FOUNDATION

Dear Andy:

I was a little nervous about sharing the story with you. When my son, Ryan, was diagnosed with AIDS in 1984, our entire world changed. We were befriended by celebrities, shunned by Ryan's school and forced into the public eye by the media. Reactions ranged from total support to total rejection.

But my greatest disappointment came at the hands of my best friend. We had been friends since grade school, nearly thirty years. When my friend found out Ryan had AIDS she began to withdraw from us. Her children couldn't play with my children. She no longer wanted to visit me. When I needed a friend more than ever, she wasn't there for me.

At first I was hurt. I was angry. How could my best friend abandon me? When I got upset over the way people were treating us, Ryan would say, "They are just scared. They are trying to protect their kids like you're trying to protect me."

Now, my best friend and I are rebuilding our relationship. I learned from Ryan that good people sometimes do bad things because they need education. That's why I started The Ryan White Foundation—to educate people about HIV and AIDS. If we do our jobs, other families won't lose their friends because of ignorance and fear.

Sincerely,

Jeanne White

Jeanne White

Andy Andrews

Andy Andrews has been inspiring people for over two decades. He is an author, entertainer, speaker, and comedian. He has spoken to millions of people–including four Presidents of the United States!

Dear Friend,

I found out early in my life that if you don't give up hope, good news is right around the corner! Sometimes, bad things happen to good people. As you can see by the letters in this book, successful people have problems, too.

One difference between successful people and everyone else is that the successful people never seem to quit. Even when times are tough, they smile and keep going. That is why they have become people we admire. Successful people have great attitudes–just like you!

Won't it be terrific to grow up and see yourself in a book like this? I CAN'T WAIT TO READ YOUR STORY! GO FOR IT!

Your friend,

Andy Andrews

In Your Own Words

Do you have your own story about how you NEVER GAVE UP you'd like to share with Andy? Use this letter to tell Andy how you've learned to keep trying, to believe in your dreams, and to never give up. Maybe you'll spot your letter in one of Andy's future books!

Dear Andy,

Ask an adult to help you cut out this letter. Put your letter in an addressed, stamped envelope and send it to: Andy Andrews, Never Give Up and Go For It, PO Box 17321, Nashville, TN, 37217 or go to: www.AndyAndrews.com.

DRAW A PICTURE OF A
HERO IN YOUR LIFE,
OR A HERO YOU WOULD LIKE
TO BE SOMEDAY!

DO YOU BELIEVE IN ANGELS? WRITE ABOUT THEM.

WRITE ABOUT AN INSPIRATIONAL HERO IN YOUR LIFE!

Early Reader Tips
From Dalmatian Press

The DALMATIAN PRESS EARLY READER SERIES offers a perfect opportunity to teach children ages 6 through 10 to explore the wonderful world of reading. To inspire you, here are some great tips from Dalmatian Press, a publisher devoted to enriching the lives of children and their families through the magical experience of books. A lifelong love of reading awaits you!

MAKE READING A PART OF EVERY DAY:

* Let children help you choose their books.
* If reading time gives way to other activities, now is the time to restore its proper place in your child's life. As you schedule activities, be sure to include time to find books at the library or from your local store where books are sold.
* When you set bedtimes, build in time for reading.
* Studies agree that reading aloud is the single most important thing a child can do to better succeed in school. Books from Dalmatian Press offer the excitement, character development, and vocabulary that make reading aloud fun.

REASSURE CHILDREN:

* As children grow up, they often find new activities difficult or intimidating. Reassure them by reading about characters who share similar experiences from the DALMATIAN PRESS EARLY READER SERIES .

MAKE IT SPECIAL:

* Have a special place where children can keep their books.
* Talk with children about what they are reading. This sends the message that you think reading is important and gives children the chance to reflect on what they've been reading.
* Finally, **have fun** with reading – today and every day!